JAPANESE FASHIONS

Ming Ju-Sun

DOVER PUBLICATIONS, INC.
Mineola, N.Y.

INTRODUCTION

The fashions in this book illustrate traditional Japanese clothing styles between 1338 and 1912. Arranged here according to Japan's historical and political eras, the clothing reflects the subtle modifications the Japanese made to their ancient garb (short of adopting Western dress) which enabled them to function in the global community at the beginning of the 20th century.

When the power of Japan's ancient imperial court flagged in the middle of the 9th century, the *shogun*, a line of military governors, assumed civil power. In 1338, Ashikaga Takauji seized control of the government, founding a dynasty that lasted 250 years. The Ashikaga family was overthrown in 1573.

By 1600, the Tokugawa family had established a new *bakufu*, or military government. This family, which maintained strict feudal controls, is remembered for the dramatic cultural and economic changes that took place in Japan under its rule.

The delicate balance of power held by the Tokugawa family was upset by the introduction of Western technology into Japan, resulting in the resignation of the *shogun* in 1867. Taking political control, the Meiji Restoration reinstated Imperial rule, which transformed the country into a modern state. While Japan was defeated in World War II (1945), it has emerged from the ashes as one of the most important economic powers in the world.

Bibliographical Note

Japanese Fashions is a new work, first published by Dover Publications, Inc., in 1999.

DOVER *Pictorial Archive* SERIES

International Standard Book Number: 0-486-40569-9

Manufactured in the United States of America
Dover Publications, Inc., 31 East 2nd Street, Mineola, N.Y. 11501

Ashikaga Period (1338–1573)

The ceremonial costume worn by this court lady is comprised of many silk robes which have been layered. Each robe has very wide sleeves; the bow at her waist has long, flowing ends which trail to the floor.

Ashikaga Period
This formally dressed lady of the court wears 12 lightweight silk robes, each a different shade.

Ashikaga Period
This woman and man, both commoners, wear everyday
kimonos and sandals. Her skirt is wrapped; his loose trousers
are tied at the waist with a sash.

Ashikaga Period

These female street vendors are selling small fish and candies which they carry in baskets. Their *kimonos* are tied at the waists with sashes; their hats are made from pieces of cloth that have been wrapped and tied.

8

Ashikaga Period

This nobleman of the court wears a formal summer costume comprised of a wide-sleeved robe with a trailing train, an embroidered, fringed sash, and wide-legged trousers. The hat denotes his rank.

Ashikaga Period

A lady of the court wears an everyday summer costume. Made of silk, it consists of two robes covering a *kimono*.

The skirt is tied at the waist; the large bow has flowing ends. Her long, straight hair is held back by a ribbon.

10

Ashikaga Period

The vestment worn by this Buddhist prince is a
brocade robe. It is wrapped with a square-shaped piece of
cloth, indicating that he is a priest.

Ashikaga Period

This upper-class boy wears everyday clothing. His robe has very wide sleeves trimmed with double rows of ribbon. He also wears pleated, loose-fitting pants that are tied at the waist.

Momoyama Period (1568–1603)
This woman, from the upper warrior class, wears a ceremonial outfit. The outer robe, which is richly embroidered,
covers 2 layers of *kimonos,* and is tied at the waist by a sash.

Momoyama Period
In formal dress, this woman from the upper warrior class
wears many layers of robes over *kimonos*.

Momoyama Period

This peasant woman, selling firewood, wears a cotton outer *kimono* covering her under *kimono*. She also wears gloves, leg coverings, straw sandals, and a cloth on her head.

Momoyama Period
Here is a street peddler dressed in loose trousers with side openings, a cotton *kimono* decorated with a geometric motif, leg coverings, and sandals.

Momoyama Period

This warrior wears armor with shoulder and arm plates, and gloves. His pleated, wide-leg trousers are tucked into shin guards. Patterned socks with sandals cover his feet. He is equipped with a sword and a dagger.

Momoyama Period
This entertainer wears a colorful *kimono*. The tasseled
cord which wraps around her waist is tied in a bow.

18

Momoyama Period

Here is an upper-class woman dressed for travel. The large straw hat and hemp veil offer her protection from the elements. A purse hangs from a cord around her neck.

Momoyama Period

Shown here is a warrior wearing an everyday costume comprised of pleated trousers and a jacket with sleeves detailed with cord. His son wears armor and a robe with double rows of ribbon at the sleeve openings. The child's pleated trousers are tied at the ankles.

Momoyama Period

This lady of the warrior class wears a formal summer costume. The elaborately embroidered outer robe, which is draped around her waist, covers an outer *kimono* and 2 under *kimonos*. A bow holds back her long hair.

Momoyama Period
This man is a general from the warrior class. His every-day outfit consists of a jacket with large sleeves, pleated trousers, and a matching sash.

Momoyama Period

Here is a *Shinto* priest on a missionary tour. He wears pleated trousers, an outer robe with a full-length back, and free-flowing panels in front.

Momoyama Period
This soldier, his torso protected with armor, also wears
short trousers with narrow legs, leg guards, and sandals.

Edo Period (1603–1868)

On the left is an upper-class woman dressed in a small-sleeved *kimono*. Her friend, on the right, is a married woman of the same rank. She wears a walking costume.

Edo Period
This woman, a commoner, wears a small-sleeved *kimono*
and *obi,* or wide sash. Her hair is adorned with ribbons and
a comb.

Edo Period

These 2 commoners are traveling. The man on the left wears a short cape while his friend wears a short coat. Both men wear gloves, leggings, socks and sandals, and carry straw hats. Their belongings, which are carefully wrapped, hang over their shoulders.

Edo Period
To play football, this man wears a *kimono* jacket with
voluminous sleeves. His loose trousers are tied at the waist
with braided silk cords and tassels.

Edo Period

Here is a young dancer wearing an elaborate costume with long, swinging sleeves and a geometric, patterned sash across her chest. Her *kimono* is decorated with flower and water designs; her hair is adorned with branches of leaves.

Edo Period
Playing a leading role in a Japanese *No* play, this dancer
portrays the character of a goddess by wearing the mask of
a young girl.

Edo Period
A bride of the upper merchant class, this young woman wears a traditional wedding ensemble consisting of an embroidered outer coat, a *kimono,* and an *obi.*

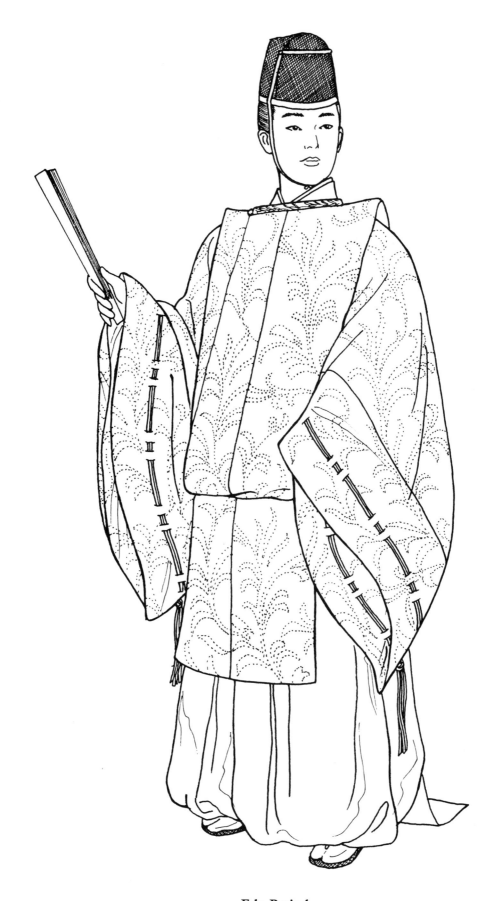

Edo Period
This high-ranking *samurai* is wearing a ceremonial robe
with a small train and voluminous trousers.

Edo Period

On the left is a young housemaid wearing a cotton *kimono,* an *obi,* and wooden platform sandals. Her mistress, on the right, who is a commoner, wears a small-sleeved *kimono* and an *obi.*

Edo Period

This young woman, a commoner, wears an everyday *kimono* decorated with a floral design and wrapped with a simple sash.

Edo Period
Here is a military officer at court wearing a ceremonial summer robe with a long train, and loose trousers tucked into his boots. A decorative, fringed sash is tied at his waist.

Edo Period

Wearing an outer coat, a *kimono*, pleated wide-legged trousers, and socks, this *samurai* carries a sword, and a dagger. A falcon is perched on his hand.

Meiji Period
This man, a middle ranking government official, wears a
ceremonial costume robe, a vest, a fringed sash, a feathered
hat, and trousers tucked into his leg guards.

Meiji Period

With tighter sleeves, a shorter jacket and skirt, and a fur hat, the uniform worn by this officer of the Royal Army has an updated look which has been influenced by Western military styles.

Meiji Period

Here is a married woman, a commoner, who wears a small-sleeved *kimono* called a *kosode*, and an *obi* tied with a cord. Her simple hairstyle has minimal adornment.

Meiji Period

This flower vendor wears traditional clothing. The sleeves of her cotton jacket are held back with a ribbon to allow for mobility. She wears an apron at the waist as well as gloves, leggings, and a cloth to protect her head.

Meiji Period

This lady-in-waiting at the Imperial Palace wears a ceremonial costume comprised of outer robes and a wide-legged trouser/skirt. Her sash is made from rolled ribbons and braided silk cords. Two rows of ribbons decorate the outer robe at the neck and the hem.

Meiji Period

This lady-in-waiting at the Imperial Palace wears an everyday outfit consisting of a wide-sleeved robe and a trouser/skirt. The neck, sleeve openings, and hem are decorated with 2 rows of ribbon.

Meiji Period

The Emperor is dressed for a *Shinto* ceremony. His outer robe has a long train trailing down in back. He also wears a skirt with a pleated sidepiece, wide trousers, and boots.

47